Love a Llama

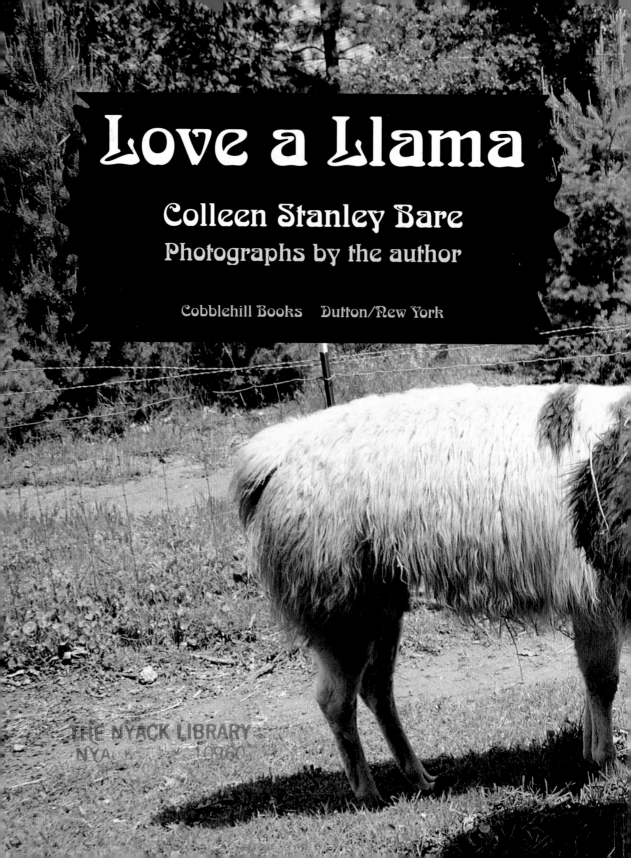

Love a Llama

Colleen Stanley Bare

Photographs by the author

Cobblehill Books   Dutton/New York

To the llama ladies:
Carolyn, Esther, Lora, the two Marys,
and Rosita.

ACKNOWLEDGMENTS

The author wishes to thank the following llama owners for their assistance and support: Esther and Paul Embree, Lora Lee Crawford, Mary Finley, Carolyn Lemmings, Rosita and Robert Richway, Roger Salter, and Mary and Rick Ulvevadet.

Library of Congress Cataloging-in-Publication Data
Bare, Colleen Stanley.
Love a llama / Colleen Stanley Bare ; photographs by the author.
    p.   cm.
    Includes index.
    Summary: Photographs and simple text introduce the physical
characteristics, habits, and natural environment of the llama.
    ISBN 0-525-65146-2
    1. Llamas—Juvenile literature.   [1. Llamas.]   I. Title.
SF401.L6B37   1994
636.2′96—dc20   92-39928   CIP   AC

Published in the United States by Cobblehill Books,
an affiliate of Dutton Children's Books,
a division of Penguin Books USA Inc.
375 Hudson Street, New York, New York 10014

Designed by Charlotte Staub
Printed in Hong Kong   First Edition
10 9 8 7 6 5 4 3 2 1

Love a llama, pat a llama, hug a llama.

But not just any llama.

Some llamas are more lovable, pattable, and huggable than other llamas.

Llamas are barnyard
animals that, with care
and training, can become
loving and friendly.

They are gentle, calm, elegant, intelligent,
and have big, beautiful eyes.

When you get near a llama, what will it do? Being very curious, it may put its face right up to your face and stare at you.

Or it may put its head on top of your head.

Or it may nudge at you and nuzzle you with its nose.

Llamas belong to the Camelidae (*camel-i-dee*) family and are close cousins of the camel. They have the soft, split upper lips and the proud look of camels, but llamas are smaller and don't have humps.

Camel

Camels can be cranky and usually aren't lovable or huggable.

Camel ancestors originated in the Central Plains of North America about 10 million years ago, later migrating to South America and Asia. Although the North American camels died out, four descendants have lived for at least six thousand years in the Andes Mountains.

Llama in South America

Alpaca

Two of these, the
llama and the alpaca,
are still raised by South American
Indians—as pack animals, pets, and for
their wool, meat, milk, and hides.

Guanaco

The other two camel relatives, the guanaco and the vicuña, live in the wild.

Llamas were first brought into the United States about a hundred years ago and today are in almost every state.

There are no wild llamas in the world.

Why do people keep llamas?

Some say llama-keeping is a "llabor of llove."

Children raise llamas as scouting, camp-fire, and 4-H farm projects.

They show them at state and county fairs and at llama shows.

The llamas are judged
for appearance and
in contests such as
obstacle-course racing.

Winning an award
is half the fun.

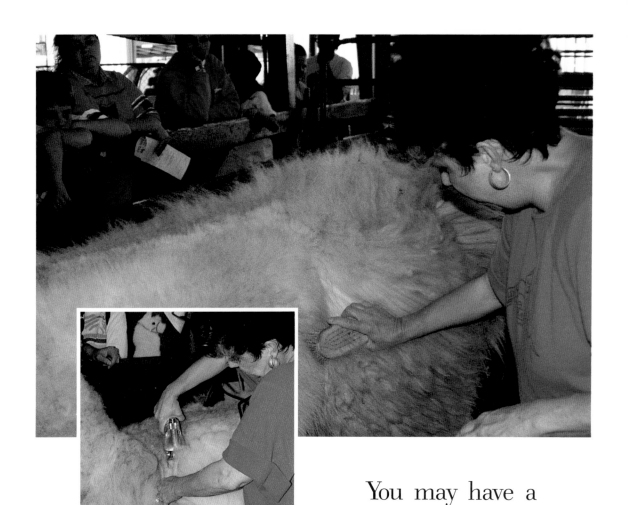

You may have a
sweater made of
soft llama hair,
because llamas are also raised for wool.

Their thick coats can be combed out or
shorn and the hair spun to make rugs,
blankets, and clothing.

Some llamas are trained to be pack animals. Hikers like to walk with llamas because they are surefooted, patient, and can carry up to one hundred pounds.

This llama is a mountain "packer."

Llamas are easy to train and can learn to follow on a long leash, called a lead, in just a few minutes.

Llamas' two-toed feet are padded underneath, so their feet don't damage trails or plants.

Llama packing is easy on the environment.

Raising llamas for sale is big business, the finest animals costing thousands of dollars.

Breeders say it is hard to give up their llamas because they are like members of the family.

Llamas are very
sociable and need
to live with at
least one other llama. Sometimes they play,
and young llamas especially like to run,
leap, and frolic.

It is fun to hand-feed a llama. They can live on hay, grasses, water, and added vitamins.

Llamas are *ruminants* (room-in-ants) like cows and sheep. This means they spend a lot of time chewing and rechewing their food, called the *cud*.

Llamas' woolly coats come in basic colors of white, black, and brown, with many color mixtures.

A baby llama may be a different color from its mother.

An adult llama weighs from 250 to 450 pounds and stands about six feet to the top of its head.

A llama female is bred at about eighteen months and will have one furry baby eleven and a half months later.

The baby is called a *cría*, meaning "baby" in Spanish. Newborns average twenty-five pounds and are able to see, hear, and walk.

The babies drink their mothers' rich milk for six months and start eating grasses at about four weeks.

Sometimes a llama mama is ill and cannot nurse her baby. Then the baby must be bottle-fed by humans, every few hours around the clock.

Occasionally a baby is born too soon, such as Dinky. Dinky weighed only sixteen pounds and was small and weak. His owner kept him inside where he nursed, slept, and grew.

Dinky

Here is Dinky a month later, alert and playful. Llamas grow quickly.

People who raise llamas have an unusual problem—what to name the new babies. Typical names are:

Candy bar names such as Hershey's Kiss, Snickers, U-No, Milky Way, Butterfinger.

Soda pop names: Coca-Cola, Pepsi, 7-Up, Dr. Pepper.

Coat color names: Blackie, Midnight, Sage, Snowflake.

Personality names: Frisky, Speedy, Sweety, Happy, Slowpoke, Hotshot, Hod-rodder, Nosy, Prince, Princess.

Can you think of some good llama names?

Llamas make sounds. They hum when they feel anxious or worried and give alarm calls if there is danger.

Llamas don't kick, bite, or buck, but they *do* spit.

When frightened or annoyed with each other, they may spit up to six feet.

But don't worry, they rarely spit at people.

The bolder, more pushy llamas become the leaders in a llama herd. They often squabble and fight to decide who will be boss.

Dominant, leader llamas eat first and may shove and spit at another llama that gets "out of line."

Llamas are bothered by flies, ticks, and worms, but they are hardy and live about twenty years.

Llama at a store promotion

Llamas get to do things that most other barnyard animals do not do.

They appear in fashion shows, store promotions, on TV, at fairs, and are used in programs for the deaf, blind, and disabled.

Llamas are invited to schools and nursing homes where they get patted and loved.

Cart pulling at a fair

Watching television

Owners often let them
inside their houses so
they will know how
to behave when they go visiting. They learn
to go up and down stairs, walk in hallways,
and to lie on the floor and watch television.

Love a llama, pat a llama, hug a llama,
For a llama can become your friend.

Llama Family Facts

Scientists have placed llamas in the scientific Class Mammalia, the Order Artiodactyla, the Suborder Tylopoda, and in the Family called Camelidae.

The Camelidae Family consists of two genera:
the Camels (*Camelus*) and the Llamas (*Lama*).

The Genus *Camelus* has two species:
Bactrian Camel (*Camelus bactrianus*), of Central Asia.
Dromedary Camel (*Camelus dromedarius*), in North Africa, Arabia, and feral in Australia.

The Genus *Lama* has four species, originally found in the high Andes Mountains of South America. Today they are in parts of Peru, Bolivia, Chile, Argentina, and Patagonia, as well as in the United States and Canada. The four species are:
Llama (*Lama glama*), pronounced LAH-MAH in English and YAH-MAH in Spanish, domesticated.
Alpaca (*Lama pacos*), AL-PACK-AH, domesticated.
Guanaco (*Lama guanicoe*), GWAH-NAH-KO, wild in South America, a few domesticated in worldwide zoos.
Vicuña (*Lama vicugna*), VY-COON-YUH, wild in South America, some domesticated in zoos of the world.

Index

DATE			